Just Enough
Difficult Topics Made Easy

Why Do Families Change?

Our First Talk About Separation and Divorce

Dr. Jillian Roberts

illustrated by

Cindy Revell

ORCA BOOK PUBLISHERS

Text copyright © Jillian Roberts 2017, 2020
Illustrations copyright © Cindy Revell 2017, 2020

Published in Canada and the United States in 2020 by Orca Book Publishers.
Previously published in 2017 by Orca Book Publishers
as a hardcover (ISBN 9781459809512).
orcabook.com

Library and Archives Canada Cataloguing in Publication
Roberts, Jillian, 1971–, author
Why do families change? : our first talk about separation
and divorce / Dr. Jillian Roberts ; illustrated by Cindy Revell.
(Just enough)
Issued in print and electronic formats.
ISBN 9781459826441 (paperback) | ISBN 9781459809529 (PDF) |
ISBN 9781459809536 (EPUB)
1. Divorce—Juvenile literature. 2. Separation (Psychology)—
Juvenile literature. I. Revell, Cindy, 1961-, illustrator II. Title.
HQ814.R62017   j306.89   C2016-904533-1
C2016-904534-X

Library of Congress Control Number: 2021937399

Summary: A nonfiction picture book that introduces very young children to
the concept of separation and divorce in a reassuring
and straightforward way.

Orca Book Publishers is committed to reducing the consumption of
nonrenewable resources in the production of our books. We make
every effort to use materials that support a sustainable future.

Orca Book Publishers gratefully acknowledges the support
for its publishing programs provided by the following
agencies: the Government of Canada, the Canada Council
for the Arts and the Province of British Columbia through
the BC Arts Council and the Book Publishing Tax Credit.

Cover and interior artwork created digitally using Corel Painter.
Cover artwork by Cindy Revell

Printed and bound in Canada.

25 24 23 22 • 3 4 5 6

For my parents.

—JR

To Terry, whose artistic nature takes the form of the
most charming of chicken houses and other creations.

—CR

Many animals in nature choose lifelong mates.

Every day, all over the world, people fall in love
and choose their own lifelong mates.

When two people fall in love, they often choose
to celebrate their love by living together.

Sometimes they get married, and sometimes they choose a common-law relationship, which means they commit to a life together without getting married.

Sometimes people stay married for the rest of their lives.

And sometimes couples who are married or in a common-law relationship get separated or divorced.

What is separation?

Separation is when a couple takes time apart from each other and their relationship. During this time, they no longer live in the same home.

After a period of separation, a married
couple may decide to get a divorce.

What is divorce?

When a couple divorces, it means they no longer
share their life and are no longer married.

If the couple has children, divorce means that there
will be changes to how the family spends time together.

Why does this happen?

People choose to separate or divorce for many different reasons. They may realize that they cannot be happy living together anymore. They might argue and make each other sad.

When people are not happy living together,
it means their home is not happy.

No matter how hard they try, sometimes
they cannot make their homes happy again.

Is it ever the kids' fault?

No. If separation or divorce happens,
it is never the fault of the children.

Do separation and divorce mean that
you are no longer a family?

Separation and divorce do not mean parents will stop loving their children. They do not mean that you stop being a family.

How do separation and divorce affect the family?

Separation and divorce mean that your family changes and looks different. Instead of having just one home, you may have two homes, and you may spend time with each of your parents in their separate homes. You may move to a different neighborhood or start at a new school.

Change also means that your parents have a chance to be happy again and to make their homes happy.

One thing that doesn't change is the love your parents and your family—your grandparents and your sisters and brothers—have for you!

What should I expect if my parents are separating or getting a divorce?

If your parents are separating or getting a divorce, know that change is coming, which can make you feel sad, scared and even angry. These feelings are normal.

What can I do to feel better?

The best way to deal with feelings is to talk about
them. Talk to someone you trust—like your parents,
a teacher, a counselor or another family member.

Ask them any questions you have. Helping create new traditions or enjoying new ways to spend time with your separated parents may help you feel better about all the changes too.

Change is difficult for everyone. While it may take some time to feel better, know that it will be okay.

Just a Few More Questions

What is custody?

Custody is a word used by lawyers and judges that means caring for and protecting someone. Parents have custody of their children when they are together. When they separate or divorce, they usually still share custody of their children—just in their separate homes.

What happens when parents don't agree on how to share custody?

Sometimes parents love their children so much it is hard for them to share their children with the other parent. Sometimes parents get angry with each other and fight with each other even after they are separated or divorced. When parents cannot agree on how to share custody, there may be a custody challenge. This means that a judge is brought in to help parents arrange a way of sharing their time with their children that avoids conflict.

What is sole custody?

Sole custody is when children live with just one parent all the time. Sometimes this happens because the other parent is not able to take proper care of them. The parent may be sick or have a job that requires a lot of travel. It is never the children's fault if one of the parents cannot look after them properly.

Will my parents get back together?

You may want your family to stay the same, but it is important to know that while your parents' decision to separate may make you very sad, it was a big decision for them that they thought a lot about, and most parents will not get back together.

What is a blended family?

A blended family is when one or both of your parents find new partners, who then become part of your family. This change can be difficult for you—it is hard to share your parents with someone else. But after a separation or divorce, it is natural for a parent to want to find another partner to help them feel happy again. This new person in your life becomes a stepmother or stepfather. If this new person has children, they become your stepsister(s) and/or stepbrother(s). When your family blends with another, your family gets bigger!

Your family may look different now, but the love they have for you will always be the same.